Arise & Shine

30-Day Devotional and Journal

KELLIE RILEY

THIS JOURNAL BELONGS TO:

IF LOST PLEASE RETURN TO OR CONTACT:

EMAIL:

PHONE:

ISBN: 978-1-7375082-2-9

DEDICATION

I want to dedicate this journal to anyone and everyone who has suffered from procrastination. May this journal motivate and inspire you to take consistent action and to execute on a higher level.

I also want to dedicate this journal to my loving husband, Mario Riley, who edited this entire project and helped me bring it to life. May this project increase our faith and encourage us to produce even more together.

Introduction:

The troubling truth is that we live in a world where most people never really do what they say they will do. The ability to self-assess or to become self-aware has seemingly become harder over the years. I recently stumbled across an incredibly thought-provoking article from the Harvard Business Review. They conducted a survey polling your average U.S. working adult and it showed that "Although, 95% of people think they're self-aware, only 10% - 15% actually are." (Harvard Business Review, 2018) What does this mean?! Well, to be self-aware means to be fully conscious of your goals, and consistent behaviors, something many are obviously lacking

This journal is an answer to this dilemma. When a person has quiet time to think, slow down, and be intentional, that's where change can happen. This journal was created for anyone who may struggle to stay focused, on task, and intentional about what they've committed to do. Inside we'll explore practical systems that I utilize myself to help me produce and complete tasks at a high level. It is also designed as a tool to assist those who love to write and express their thoughts through writing.

Anyone who knows me understands that my faith has been monumental to my success. The Word of God is one of the most powerful resources on this planet.

Therefore, the foundation of this journal is based on the Word of God. There are scriptures within this journal that have been hand selected because they have sustained me throughout the worst times in my life. Meditating on these scriptures have pushed me to keep moving, and to hold on to a good attitude and positive demeanor.

In my life, I have faced several hardships, some of which I'm sure many who pick up this journal can relate to. I know what it feels like to deal with depression, oppression, bullying, death of family member, and unfortunately death of a child. This journal helped me to keep moving forward toward my promise and destiny of my life.

I believe writing is therapeutic. I believe documentation establishes an idea and solidifies a thought. Writing is an act of authority. In contemporary today, we use written documents and contracts to conduct business. These documents and contracts rule and stand in a court of law. The authority and the power of putting pen to paper I believe is underestimated. Now, I understand we live in a digital world, but I still believe in the power of putting pen to paper.

In biblical days a King did not just speak a declaration, but it was written. The King's decree was recorded and went into effect immediately. I'm reminded in the book of Ezra when the King Xeres granted Nehemiah written permission to retrieve any and all supplies needed for his mission to rebuild the temple. In other words,

Nehemiah had a blank check when it came to wood and resources. On the next page, you will find a decree, or a contract that you will be making to yourself. This will solidify your next step towards consistent change and transformation.

This Journal's Decree:

I _____ , (Your name) accept the following terms and conditions of this journal. For the next 30 days I promise to exert my best effort to follow the instructions of this journal and to complete this assignment to the best of my ability.

     If I fall behind, I agree to begin again where I left off and continue to pursue this commitment to myself. If I do not complete this mission, I understand that I am allowing myself to be a part of that 95% of people who do not follow through. In other words, I am not a person of my word. If I find myself not being productive within the following 4 weeks, the consequences will be:

1.) _____

2.) _____

This is the commitment I am making to myself. At the end of this 30-day journal I will be more self-aware, productive, and secure in my faith.

Sincerely,

_____

(Your Signature Here)

Instructions for Arise & Shine
30-Day Transformational Journal:

The following instructions are provided to help the reader complete this journal with accuracy. Below you will find a breakdown on how to complete each page presented repeatedly on the different days. Each page was designed intentionally to allow the reader to receive uplifting messages of hope, along with pages to contemplate and express the journalist's emotions.

INTIAL DAY PAGES:

At the beginning of every DAY there will be an inspirational scripture presented to read. It is encouraged for the reader to read the chapter and verse, but to also take time to read the entire chapter for context. Below every scripture you will see a section labeled as "Coach Kellie's Corner."

Kellie's Corner contains her revelation of the scripture provided. She will express her opinion, experience on the scripture, along with definitions of selected words. Kellie believes understanding the Word of God is so essential and key to transformation and productivity.

MEDITATION PAGES: (These pages should be completed in the morning)

Meditation pages are provided for each day of this 30-day journal. These pages are designated for the reader to write their interpretation of the text. The reader is encouraged to write their thoughts on the definitions and revelation provided. How can this scripture be applied to life today? What are some practical things I can take away from this message of hope?

PRODUCTIVITY PAGES: (These pages should be completed in the morning)

Productivity pages are given to allow the reader to prioritize important items to complete each day. The left column of the productivity page is designed to direct the reader to "brain dump." The concept of brain dumping is the practice of writing down all thoughts, tasks, and goals to be completed. These tasks should be SMART. Specific, Measurable, Attainable, Realistic, and Timely.

The purpose of this process is to prevent over thinking and the emotions of feeling overwhelmed. Once all tasks, obligations, and commitments have been written down, it will assist in clearing the mind to prioritize. The right column is designed to narrow down 3 to 5 items that can be executed or completed on that day.

Kellie believes that completing small tasks everyday helps create motion and momentum to cultivate productivity. The foundation of the Word of God along with action and consistent movement is POWERFUL. The reader should be intentional to complete these items and to not fall stagnant.

REFLECTION PAGES: (These pages should be completed in the evening)

Reflection pages are designed for expression of thought at the end of the day.

Any epiphanies received and provoking notions should be recorded. I believe expressing your opinion through writing can be therapeutic. One thing I enjoy about writing in my journal is that the book doesn't have the capability to speak or prejudge what is being written. I am able to transfer energy whether good or bad onto the page to help me process what I am experiencing at the moment.

DREAM PAGES/ EXTRA:

If you are a dreamer like myself, I have provided extra pages for you to document your dreams. Also, extra pages for those exciting moments and days filled with blessings and testimonies that must be recorded.

Month: # Year:

Sunday	Monday	Tuesday	Wednesday	Thursday	Friday	Saturday

NOTES:
_____

_____

DAY 1

"Arise [from spiritual depression to a new life], shine [be radiant with the glory and brilliance of the LORD]; for your light has come, And the glory and brilliance of the LORD has risen upon you. ²For in fact, darkness will cover the earth, And deep darkness will cover the peoples; But the LORD will rise upon you [Jerusalem] And His glory and brilliance will be seen on you."

Isaiah 60: 1-2 AMP

Coach Kellie's Corner:

This scripture is so near and dear to my heart. ARISE and SHINE. Arise meaning to make a conscious decision to get up and embrace a new life.

Arise is a verb meaning: to begin, to occur, or to exist: to come into being or to attention.

The amplified version tells us to arise from spiritual depression to a new life. How powerful, did you know a new start can come from a dark place? I believe the darkness gives us a new canvas to shine upon. Shine like a star and show the world how unique and authentic you truly are. It is your time; your light has come. In the midst of darkness and chaos, make a deliberate decision to radiate. The text reminds us that there will be thick darkness on the Earth; however, let's have the audacity to illuminate in the midst of it. Isaiah reminds us that God's glory and brilliance will be seen on you. Yes you! Your inner genius and wisdom will be on display for all to see.

DAY ONE: MEDITATION   DATE: _____.

Take a moment to journal what this scripture means to you. Meditate on the text. I encourage you to read the entire chapter. How can you apply this text to where you are today?

_____

_____

_____

_____

_____

_____

_____

_____

_____

_____

_____

DAY ONE: PRODUCTIVITY PAGE

Take a moment to write down every task that may be on your mind during this moment. This section will be called the "Brain Dump". We will prioritize on the next column. In order to execute at a high level, prioritization must always be key.

Now out of that list of items that have been written down and off your mind. Prioritize and narrow down at least 3 task you can complete today!

Allow each task to be SMART. Specific, Measurable, Attainable, Realistic, and Timely (Complete Today). Don't allow yourself to be too ambitious, we achieve major progress by completing small steps daily. Once the task has been completed, check the complete box.

_____

_____

_____

☐ Completed

_____

_____

_____

_____

☐ Completed

_____

_____

_____

_____

☐ Completed

DAY ONE: REFLECTION   DATE: _____.

Take a moment to journal and reflect on your day. Did you remember to RISE and
SHINE? (Isaiah 60: 1-2) Let's take a moment to consider the events of today and
document what occurred.

_____

_____

_____

_____

_____

_____

_____

_____

_____

_____

_____

_____

DAY 2

"God always gives you all the grace you need. So you will only have to suffer for a little while. Then God himself will build you up again. He will make you strong and steady. And he has chosen you to share in his eternal glory because you belong to Christ."
1 Peter 5:10 NIRV

Coach Kellie's Corner:

This scripture reminds us of God's unfailing grace that is assigned to our lives. Our father's constant goodness that follows us even when we don't deserve it.

The definition of Grace is listed as courteous goodwill:

Peter warns us that in this life there are some obstacles we will have to endure, that we all have moments of suffering. However, the pain will only be momentary and that God himself will rescue you.

One definition of Build to is make stronger or more intense:

He promises to make us strong and steady, not just to endure life. The text conveys that He hand selected us to contribute and be a part of His glory. We belong to Him, and He promises to take care of us. Glory to God!

DAY TWO: MEDITATION   DATE: _____.

Take a moment to journal what this scripture means to you. Meditate on the text. I encourage you to read the entire chapter. How can you apply this text to where you are today?

_____

_____

_____

_____

_____

_____

_____

_____

_____

_____

_____

DAY TWO: PRODUCTIVITY PAGE

Take a moment to write down every task that may be on your mind during this moment. This section will be called the "Brain Dump" We will prioritize on the next column. In order to execute at a high level, prioritization must always be key.

Now out of that list of items that have been written down and off your mind. Prioritize and narrow down at least 3 task you can complete today!

Allow each task to be SMART. Specific, Measurable, Attainable, Realistic, and Timely (Complete Today). Don't allow yourself to be too ambitious, we achieve major progress by completing small steps daily. Once the task has been completed, check the complete box.

_____

_____

_____

☐ Completed

_____

_____

☐ Completed

_____

_____

☐ Completed

DAY TWO: REFLECTION

DATE: _____.

Take a moment to journal and reflect on your day. Did you remember that you have God's GRACE assigned to your life? (1Peter 5:10 NIRV) Let's take a moment to consider the events of today and document what occurred.

_____

_____

_____

_____

_____

_____

_____

_____

_____

_____

_____

_____

_____

_____

_____

_____

_____

_____

_____

_____

_____

_____

_____

_____

_____

DAY 3

"I am convinced and confident of this very thing, that He who has begun a good work in you will [continue to] perfect and complete it until the day of Christ Jesus [the time of His return]."
Philippians 1:6 AMP

Coach Kellie's Corner:

This scripture has definitely encouraged me on some of the darkness days of my life. In life sometimes it is easy to lose sight of the promise and fall victim of those persistence negative thoughts we all have. However, this text reminds to never lose hope and to be assured and confident in God.

The definition of convinced is listed as completely certain about something:

It goes on to tell us to that not only will He deliver on his promise, but He will not stop until it is perfect! We probably have all experienced working with someone that does the bare minimum. Someone who is known to get the job done, but maybe misses a few details, that's not God.

One definition of perfect is having all the required or desirable elements, qualities, or characteristics as good as it is possible to be:

Look at how our God operates. He will not rest until ALL required and desired elements have been collected and considered. Be encouraged today.

DAY THREE: MEDITATION

DATE: _____.

Take a moment to journal what this scripture means to you. Meditate on the text. I encourage you to read the entire chapter. How can you apply this text to where you are today?

_____

_____

_____

_____

_____

_____

_____

_____

_____

_____

_____

_____

DAY THREE: PRODUCTIVITY PAGE

Take a moment to write down every task that may be on your mind during this moment. This section will be called the "Brain Dump". We will prioritize on the next column. In order to execute at a high level, prioritization must always be key.

Now out of that list of items that have been written down and off your mind. Prioritize and narrow down at least 3 task you can complete today!

Allow each task to be SMART. Specific, Measurable, Attainable, Realistic, and Timely (Complete Today). Don't allow yourself to be too ambitious, we achieve major progress by completing small steps daily. Once the task has been completed, check the complete box.

_____

_____

_____

_____ ☐ Completed

_____

_____

_____ ☐ Completed

_____

_____

_____ ☐ Completed

DAY THREE: REFLECTION   DATE: _____.

Take a moment to journal and reflect on your day. Did you stay confident in God? He is perfecting every situation. (Philippians 1:6 AMP) Let's take a moment to consider the events of today and document what occurred.

_____

_____

_____

_____

_____

_____

_____

_____

_____

_____

_____

_____

DAY 4

"But as for me, I will wait and hope continually, And will praise You yet more and more." Psalms 71:14 AMP

"But I will always have hope. I will praise you more and more." Psalms 71:14 GW

<u>Coach Kellie's Corner:</u>

Some believers may be under the impression that the enemy is after your finances or that the attack is geared toward your job or dreams and aspirations. However, I believe the greatest attack will always be geared toward your faith. The enemy doesn't want you to believe things will be better. He wants you to focus on the negative and rehearse it over and over in your mind. Faith is a weapon we use to fight with. Remember faith is everything to God, without faith it is impossible to please Him.

We are encouraged from above to always have faith and to wait patiently on the Lord. Just like the psalm says; when times get tough, we should praise Him even more. When the intensity of the storm rises, our praise should rise as well. Our focus should remain on what is working, what is good, and what God is able and about to do!

DAY FOUR: MEDITATION   DATE: _____.

Take a moment to journal what this scripture means to you. Meditate on the text. I encourage you to read the entire chapter. How can you apply this text to where you are today?

_____

_____

_____

_____

_____

_____

_____

_____

_____

_____

_____

DAY FOUR: PRODUCTIVITY PAGE

Take a moment to write down every task that may be on your mind during this moment. This section will be called the "Brain Dump". We will prioritize on the next column. In order to execute at a high level, prioritization must always be key.

Now out of that list of items have been written down and off your mind. Prioritize and narrow down at least 3 task you can complete today!

Allow each task to be SMART. Specific, Measurable, Attainable, Realistic, and Timely (Complete Today). Don't allow yourself to be too ambitious, we complete major progress by completely small steps daily. Once the task has been completed, check the complete box.

_____

_____

_____

☐ Completed

_____

_____

_____

_____

☐ Completed

_____

_____

_____

☐ Completed

DAY FOUR: REFLECTION   DATE: _____.

Take a moment to journal and reflect on your day. Remember your praise and hope must stay in the forefront. (Psalms 71:14 AMP) Let's take a moment to consider the events of today and document what occurred.

_____

_____

_____

_____

_____

_____

_____

_____

_____

_____

_____

_____

_____

_____

_____

_____

_____

_____

_____

_____

_____

_____

_____

_____

_____

DAY 5

"Many there are that say of my soul,

There is no help for him in God. [Selah]

But thou, O Jehovah, art a shield about me;

My glory, and the lifter up of my head.

I cry unto Jehovah with my voice,

And he answereth me out of his holy hill. [Selah}

I laid me down and slept;

I awaked; for Jehovah sustaineth me."

Psalms 3:2-5 ASV

Coach Kellie's Corner:

I personally like when people underestimate me. However, it is another thing to underestimate God. The psalm talks about many people in this text doubting the ability of God in this particular situation. Yet God is our shield, our glory, and most definitely the encourager who lifts our head.

Glory: high renown or honor won by notable achievements. Another definition says magnificence or great beauty.

We live in a world unfortunately where people can see you cry and feel no remorse. Yet, God not only hears your cry but He does something about it. The Lord is truly our savior and sustainer.

DAY FIVE: MEDITATION

DATE: _____.

Take a moment to journal what this scripture means to you. Meditate on the text. I encourage you to read the entire chapter. How can you apply this text to where you are today?

_____

_____

_____

_____

_____

_____

_____

_____

_____

_____

DAY FIVE: PRODUCTIVITY PAGE

Take a moment to write down every task that may be on your mind during this moment. This section will be called the "Brain Dump". We will prioritize on the next column. In order to execute at a high level, prioritization must always be key.

Now out of that list of items that have been written down and off your mind. Prioritize and narrow down at least 3 task you can complete today!

Allow each task to be SMART. Specific, Measurable, Attainable, Realistic, and Timely (Complete Today). Don't allow yourself to be too ambitious, we achieve major progress by completing small steps daily. Once the task has been completed, check the complete box.

_____

_____

_____

_____

☐ Completed

_____

_____

_____

☐ Completed

_____

_____

☐ Completed

_____

DAY FIVE: REFLECTION   DATE: _____.

Take a moment to journal and reflect on your day. God is our great sustainer. (Psalms 3:2-5 ASV) Let's take a moment to consider the events of today and document what occurred.

_____

_____

_____

_____

_____

_____

_____

_____

_____

_____

_____

_____

_____

_____

_____

_____

_____

_____

_____

_____

_____

_____

_____

DAY 6

"For our momentary light affliction is producing for us an absolutely incomparable eternal weight of glory. So we do not focus on what is seen, but on what is unseen. For what is seen is temporary, but what is unseen is eternal."

2 Corinthians 4:17-18 CSB

Coach Kellie's Corner:

We all go through trials and tribulations. During those times, we don't always think about what could be behind the struggle or test. The scripture reminds us to focus on the glory that is coming after the storm. Sometimes it's hard to understand that each affliction is working for us, making us stronger, wiser, and overall better human beings. The key is to shift the focus from the trial to an outcome of victory. I remind myself often, light affliction equals heavy glory. A little dilemma to overcome, eternal weight of splendor. For what we see now is only temporary because we live in the moment, but the unseen future will hold victory.

DAY SIX: MEDITATION

DATE: _____.

Take a moment to journal what this scripture means to you. Meditate on the text. I encourage you to read the entire chapter. How can you apply this text to where you are today?

_____

_____

_____

_____

_____

_____

_____

_____

_____

_____

DAY SIX: PRODUCTIVITY PAGE

Take a moment to write down every task that may be on your mind during this moment. This section will be called the "Brain Dump". We will prioritize on the next column. In order to execute at a high level, prioritization must always be key.

_____

_____

_____

_____

_____

_____

_____

_____

_____

Now out of that list of items that have been written down and off your mind. Prioritize and narrow down at least 3 task you can complete today!

Allow each task to be SMART. Specific, Measurable, Attainable, Realistic, and Timely (Complete Today). Don't allow yourself to be too ambitious, we achieve major progress by completing small steps daily. Once the task has been completed, check the complete box.

_____

_____

☐ Completed

_____

_____

☐ Completed

_____

☐ Completed

DAY SIX: REFLECTION   DATE: _____.

Take a moment to journal and reflect on your day. Let's stay focused on glory. (2 Corinthians 4:17) Take a moment to consider the events of today and document what occurred.

_____

_____

_____

_____

_____

_____

_____

_____

_____

_____

_____

DAY 7

"The LORD is my strength and my [impenetrable] shield;
My heart trusts [with unwavering confidence] in Him, and I am helped;
Therefore, my heart greatly rejoices,
And with my song I shall thank Him and praise Him."
Psalms 28:7 AMP

Coach Kellie's Corner:

In life there will be times that we have to tap into a greater strength. It's important that we know that God is for us and we must trust Him. I remember times of consecration and fasting, so much would be exposed. I don't know if we realize how much unbelief we may have or may be holding on to. Therefore, learning to trust in God is the key.

The text reminds us to trust in Him, have confidence and we will be helped. So praise him in advance as an activation of faith and validation of trust. Remember, the bible tells us the joy of the Lord will always be our strength.

DAY SEVEN: MEDITATION   DATE: _____.

Take a moment to journal what this scripture means to you. Meditate on the text. I encourage you to read the entire chapter. How can you apply this text to where you are today?

_____

_____

_____

_____

_____

_____

_____

_____

_____

_____

_____

DAY SEVEN: PRODUCTIVITY PAGE

Take a moment to write down every task that may be on your mind during this moment. This section will be called the "Brain Dump". We will prioritize on the next column. In order to execute at a high level, prioritization must always be key.

Now out of that list of items that have been written down and off your mind. Prioritize and narrow down at least 3 task you can complete today!

Allow each task to be SMART. Specific, Measurable, Attainable, Realistic, and Timely (Complete Today). Don't allow yourself to be too ambitious, we achieve major progress by completing small steps daily. Once the task has been completed, check the complete box.

_____

_____

_____

☐ Completed

_____

_____

_____

_____

_____

☐ Completed

_____

_____

_____

_____

☐ Completed

DAY SEVEN: REFLECTION   DATE: _____.

Take a moment to journal and reflect on your day. Did you remember to trust God and praise him today? (Psalms 28:7 AMP) Let's take a moment to consider the events of today and document what occurred.

_____

_____

_____

_____

_____

_____

_____

_____

_____

_____

_____

_____

_____

_____

_____

_____

_____

_____

_____

_____

_____

_____

_____

_____

Well Done!

Job well done on completing one week of consistently journaling your transformation progress. Let's continue to move forward, reflect on your progress. My hope is that you are gaining momentum.

What scripture did you connect with the most this week? Why?

_____

_____

What were your wins for the week? What were you able to complete?

_____

_____

What are your grateful for going into next week?

_____

_____

You have one week under your belt, lets finish the next 3 strong!

WEEK 1 COMPLETE

DAY 8

"Don't be afraid, because I am with you. Don't be intimidated; I am your God. I will strengthen you. I will help you. I will support you with my victorious right hand." - Isaiah 41:10 GW

"Do not fear [anything], for I am with you; Do not be afraid, for I am your God. I will strengthen you, be assured I will help you; I will certainly take hold of you with My righteous right hand [a hand of justice, of power, of victory, of salvation]." - Isaiah 41:10 AMP

Coach Kellie's Corner:

Intimidation is real, and fear can cause you to freeze and tense up. There are many times where I have felt overwhelmed and intimidated. One definition for intimidation is:

to have a frightening, overawing, or threatening effect.

However, our God tells us to not be frightened or threatened by anything. He will help us and strengthen us, give us victory and power. In a world that is undeniably unpredictable we can rest in knowing God will help us and give us power.

DAY EIGHT: MEDITATION   DATE: _____.

Take a moment to journal what this scripture means to you. Meditate on the text. I encourage you to read the entire chapter. How can you apply this text to where you are today?

_____

_____

_____

_____

_____

_____

_____

_____

_____

_____

_____

_____

DAY EIGHT: PRODUCTIVITY PAGE

Take a moment to write down every task that may be on your mind during this moment. This section will be called the "Brain Dump". We will prioritize on the next column. In order to execute at a high level, prioritization must always be key.

Now out of that list of items that have been written down and off your mind. Prioritize and narrow down at least 3 task you can complete today!

Allow each task to be SMART. Specific, Measurable, Attainable, Realistic, and Timely (Complete Today). Don't allow yourself to be too ambitious, we achieve major progress by completing small steps daily. Once the task has been completed, check the complete box.

_____

_____

_____

☐ Completed

_____

_____

_____

_____

☐ Completed

_____

_____

_____

☐ Completed

_____

DAY EIGHT: REFLECTION   DATE: _____.

Take a moment to journal and reflect on your day. Know that you're not alone and you have help and power. (Isaiah 41:10) Let's take a moment to consider the events of today and document what occurred.

_____

_____

_____

_____

_____

_____

_____

_____

_____

_____

_____

DAY 9

"Finally, believers, whatever is true, whatever is honorable and worthy of respect, whatever is right and confirmed by God's word, whatever is pure and wholesome, whatever is lovely and brings peace, whatever is admirable and of good repute; if there is any excellence, if there is anything worthy of praise, think continually on these things [center your mind on them, and implant them in your heart]."
Philippians 4:8 AMP

Coach Kellie's Corner:

It is a scientific fact that over 80% of our thoughts are negative. It doesn't take much to worry or to overthink any matter we may be facing. This is why we must be intentional on focusing on things that are lovely, peaceful, and of good report. I believe our thoughts are tunnels and they can lead in a positive or negative direction. The bible tells us here to center your mind, think continually about the goodness of God. Remember there is power in your praise, that praise is literally a weapon to keep us in a state of gratefulness and it deters depression. Have you ever tried to complain and praise God at the same time? It's hard. I don't believe you can sincerely do both at the same time. Remember, let's be intentional about our thoughts and implant the positive ones in our hearts. David was the one who stated I will hide thy word in my heart, that I might not sin against you Lord.

DAY NINE: MEDITATION

DATE: _____.

Take a moment to journal what this scripture means to you. Meditate on the text. I encourage you to read the entire chapter. How can you apply this text to where you are today?

_____

_____

_____

_____

_____

_____

_____

_____

_____

_____

_____

DAY NINE: PRODUCTIVITY PAGE

Take a moment to write down every task that may be on your mind during this moment. This section will be called the "Brain Dump". We will prioritize on the next column. In order to execute at a high level, prioritization must always be key.

Now out of that list of items that have been written down and off your mind. Prioritize and narrow down at least 3 task you can complete today!

Allow each task to be SMART. Specific, Measurable, Attainable, Realistic, and Timely (Complete Today). Don't allow yourself to be too ambitious, we achieve major progress by completing small steps daily. Once the task has been completed, check the complete box.

_____

_____

☐ Completed

_____

_____

☐ Completed

_____

_____

☐ Completed

DAY NINE: REFLECTION   DATE: _____.

Take a moment to journal and reflect on your day. Did your positive or negative thoughts dominate today? (Philippians 4:8) Let's take a moment to consider the events of today and document what occurred.

_____

_____

_____

_____

_____

_____

_____

_____

_____

_____

_____

DAY 10

"For the one who sows to his flesh [his sinful capacity, his worldliness, his disgraceful impulses] will reap from the flesh ruin and destruction, but the one who sows to the Spirit will from the Spirit reap eternal life. Let us not grow weary or become discouraged in doing good, for at the proper time we will reap, if we do not give in. So then, while we [as individual believers] have the opportunity, let us do good to all people [not only being helpful, but also doing that which promotes their spiritual well-being], and especially [be a blessing] to those of the household of faith (born-again believers)."
Galatians 6: 8-10 AMP

Coach Kellie's Corner:

Anyone can start a project and never finish. Many people can begin a hobby or new workout routine and stop after a couple of weeks. However, it takes maturity to continue to sow good seeds for years before ever seeing a harvest. Discipline and consistency will forever be two determining factors in reaping a harvest or accomplishing a goal. The Bible reminds us to not become discouraged, when it comes to discipline emotions and feelings have to take a back seat. The principle assures us that we will receive the victory if we remain in faith and stay consistent.

DAY TEN: MEDITATION

DATE: _____.

Take a moment to journal what this scripture means to you. Meditate on the text. I encourage you to read the entire chapter. How can you apply this text to where you are today?

_____

_____

_____

_____

_____

_____

_____

_____

_____

_____

_____

_____

DAY TEN: PRODUCTIVITY PAGE

Take a moment to write down every task that may be on your mind during this moment. This section will be called the "Brain Dump". We will prioritize on the next column. In order to execute at a high level, prioritization must always be key.

Now out of that list of items that have been written down and off your mind. Prioritize and narrow down at least 3 task you can complete today!

Allow each task to be SMART. Specific, Measurable, Attainable, Realistic, and Timely (Complete Today). Don't allow yourself to be too ambitious, we achieve major progress by completing small steps daily. Once the task has been completed, check the complete box.

_____

_____

_____

☐ Completed

_____

_____

_____

☐ Completed

_____

_____

_____

☐ Completed

DAY TEN: REFLECTION   DATE: _____.

Take a moment to journal and reflect on your day. Remember don't grow weary in well doing. (Galatians 6:8-10AMP) Let's take a moment to consider the events of today and document what occurred.

_____

_____

_____

_____

_____

_____

_____

_____

_____

_____

_____

_____

_____

_____

_____

_____

_____

_____

_____

_____

_____

_____

_____

_____

_____

DAY 11

"Death and life are in the power of the tongue, And those who love it and indulge it will eat its fruit and bear the consequences of their words."
Proverbs 18:21 AMP

Words kill, words give life;
they're either poison or fruit—you choose.
Proverbs 18:21 MSG

Coach Kellie's Corner:

When I think about how the earth and heavens were made, the energy that went forth from God's spoken voice or words were powerful. Let there be! Words are how we express our emotions and feelings. Think about how a compliment can lift a person's demeanor and shift someone's day. This is why I personally love prophecy because it has the potential to lift and catapult someone out of a dark and difficult situation. Words can heal or hinder. When is the last time you have spoken positive affirmations over yourself or in the mirror? If you have never tried, let's start implementing that today. I can recall David from the bible stating he encouraged himself in the Lord when he had no one to do it. Never underestimate the power in our words, and let's activate that component in your life.

DAY ELEVEN: MEDITATION   DATE: _____.

Take a moment to journal what this scripture means to you. Meditate on the text. I encourage you to read the entire chapter. How can you apply this text to where you are today?

_____

_____

_____

_____

_____

_____

_____

_____

_____

_____

_____

DAY ELEVEN: PRODUCTIVITY PAGE

Take a moment to write down every task that may be on your mind during this moment. This section will be called the "Brain Dump". We will prioritize on the next column. In order to execute at a high level, prioritization must always be key.

Now out of that list of items that have been written down and off your mind. Prioritize and narrow down at least 3 task you can complete today!

Allow each task to be SMART. Specific, Measurable, Attainable, Realistic, and Timely (Complete Today). Don't allow yourself to be too ambitious, we achieve major progress by completing small steps daily. Once the task has been completed, check the complete box.

_____

_____

_____

☐ Completed

_____

_____

_____

_____

☐ Completed

_____

_____

_____

☐ Completed

DAY ELEVEN: REFLECTION   DATE: _____.

Take a moment to journal and reflect on your day. Did your words reflect life or death today? (Proverbs 18:21 AMP) Let's take a moment to consider the events of today and document what occurred.

_____

_____

_____

_____

_____

_____

_____

_____

_____

_____

_____

DAY 12

"My son, pay attention to my words and be willing to learn;

Open your ears to my sayings.

Do not let them escape from your sight;

Keep them in the center of your heart.

For they are life to those who find them,

And healing and health to all their flesh."

Proverbs 4:20 AMP

"Do not lose sight of these things.

Keep them deep within your heart

because they are life to those who find them

and they heal the whole body."

Proverbs 4:20 GW

Coach Kellie's Corner:

It is a scientific proven fact that positivity, good news, even uplifting company is good for your immune system. The positive message itself sends stimulants throughout your body that activate healing. The word of God can be equivalent to a vitamin. The scripture says its good for your spirit and for your flesh. Be encouraged to read the word every day, listen to it at night. Keep this scripture in the forefront and utilize it daily.

DAY TWELVE: MEDITATION   DATE: _____.

Take a moment to journal what this scripture means to you. Meditate on the text. I encourage you to read the entire chapter. How can you apply this text to where you are today?

_____

_____

_____

_____

_____

_____

_____

_____

_____

_____

_____

_____

DAY TWELVE: PRODUCTIVITY PAGE

Take a moment to write down every task that may be on your mind during this moment. This section will be called the "Brain Dump". We will prioritize on the next column. In order to execute at a high level, prioritization must always be key.

Now out of that list of items that have been written down and off your mind. Prioritize and narrow down at least 3 task you can complete today!

Allow each task to be SMART. Specific, Measurable, Attainable, Realistic, and Timely (Complete Today). Don't allow yourself to be too ambitious, we achieve major progress by completing small steps daily. Once the task has been completed, check the complete box.

_____

_____

_____ ☐ Completed

_____

_____

_____ ☐ Completed

_____

_____

_____ ☐ Completed

_____

DAY TWELVE: REFLECTION

DATE: _____.

Take a moment to journal and reflect on your day. Remember God's Word is good for our immune system. (Proverbs 4:20) Let's take a moment to consider the events of today and document what occurred.

_____

_____

_____

_____

_____

_____

_____

_____

_____

_____

_____

DAY 13

"However, the Lord stood by me and gave me strength so that I could finish spreading the Good News for all the nations to hear. I was snatched out of a lion's mouth. The Lord will rescue me from all harm and will take me safely to his heavenly kingdom. Glory belongs to him forever! Amen."
2 Timothy 4: 17-18 GW

Coach Kellie's Corner:

Being a believer doesn't exempt you from heartbreaking moments. I remember in some of my darkest moments, the Lord gave me strength to endure the pain. One moment I can recall is when my husband and I received devastating news about our unborn child. I remember rushing to the hospital to be informed that I was having a miscarriage. At the exact moment I had no strength at all to carry on; however, I remember God sending angels via nurses and doctors to bring comfort in the midst of my pain. I remember those mornings following, how I didn't want to get up out the bed, but the Lord would encourage me and empower me to keep going. He used different people like my son and husband to embrace me and to express how much they loved me. It was truly a supernatural strength that was placed upon me by our heavenly Father. Be encouraged today and know if you are going through a tough time right now, the same God that strengthen me will uphold you. The Lord's strength is like no other power or force on this planet. He will keep you and sustain you if you let Him. Now, I can tell my story from a place of strength, letting the world know with the Lord's help, you can get through anything.

DAY THIRTEEN: MEDITATION

DATE: _____.

Take a moment to journal what this scripture means to you. Meditate on the text. I encourage you to read the entire chapter. How can you apply this text to where you are today?

_____

_____

_____

_____

_____

_____

_____

_____

_____

_____

_____

DAY THIRTEEN: PRODUCTIVITY PAGE

Take a moment to write down every task that may be on your mind during this moment. This section will be called the "Brain Dump". We will prioritize on the next column. In order to execute at a high level, prioritization must always be key.

Now out of that list of items that have been written down and off your mind. Prioritize and narrow down at least 3 task you can complete today!

Allow each task to be SMART. Specific, Measurable, Attainable, Realistic, and Timely (Complete Today). Don't allow yourself to be too ambitious, we achieve major progress by completing small steps daily. Once the task has been completed, check the complete box.

_____

_____

_____

☐ Completed

_____

_____

_____

☐ Completed

_____

_____

_____

☐ Completed

DAY THIRTEEN: REFLECTION   DATE: _____.

Take a moment to journal and reflect on your day. Remember the Lord is our strengthener and standby. (2 Timothy 4:17-18)) Take a moment to consider the events of today and document what occurred.

_____

_____

_____

_____

_____

_____

_____

_____

_____

_____

_____

_____

DAY 14

I have told you these things, so that in Me you may have [perfect] peace. In the world you have tribulation and distress and suffering, but be courageous [be confident, be undaunted, be filled with joy]; I have overcome the world." [My conquest is accomplished, My victory abiding.]
John 16:33 AMP

I've told you this so that my peace will be with you.
In the world you'll have trouble.
But cheer up! I have overcome the world."
John 16:33 GW

Coach Kellie's Corner:

There is no doubt we are all living in turbulent times. It seems like every time I turn on the news there is a heartbreaking story about a family or a business. Jesus knew these days were approaching so he reminded us about his peace. If you are anything like me, I love peace; I appreciate and enjoy the beach, the sound of the water and the waves. I also enjoy the sounds of nature, the birds chirping, because those moments to me represent tranquility. However, there is no peace like the peace of God. Jesus was referring to this in this passage. He tells us, yes there will be trouble in the word, but you can tap into His peace that can settle any storm in your home and in your heart.

DAY FOURTEEN: MEDITATION

DATE: _____.

Take a moment to journal what this scripture means to you. Meditate on the text. I encourage you to read the entire chapter. How can you apply this text to where you are today?

_____

_____

_____

_____

_____

_____

_____

_____

_____

_____

_____

_____

DAY FOURTEEN:
PRODUCTIVITY PAGE

Take a moment to write down every task that may be on your mind during this moment. This section will be called the "Brain Dump". We will prioritize on the next column. In order to execute at a high level, prioritization must always be key.

Now out of that list of items have been written down and off your mind. Prioritize and narrow down at least 3 task you can complete today!

Allow each task to be SMART. Specific, Measurable, Attainable, Realistic, and Timely (Complete Today). Don't allow yourself to be too ambitious, we complete major progress by completely small steps daily. Once the task has been completed, check the complete box.

_____

_____

_____

_____ ☐ Completed

_____

_____

_____

_____ ☐ Completed

_____

_____ ☐ Completed

DAY FOURTEEN: REFLECTION   DATE: _____.

Take a moment to journal and reflect on your day. God's peace is with you. (John 16:33 AMP) Let's take a moment to consider the events of today and document what occurred.

_____

_____

_____

_____

_____

_____

_____

_____

_____

_____

_____

STOP!

Let's take a moment to self-assess on the progress we are making. Have you been making consistent time to journal over the past 2 weeks? Remember the purpose of this 30-day experience. The goal is to start off the day with a strong foundation of faith and hope, along with time of meditation to digest encouragement and apply it to your life.

Have you been completing your productivity pages and prioritizing your daily tasks for forward movement? Remember faith without works is dead. We must exercise our faith and put it to work. It's so easy to become overwhelmed when things aren't written down, even the smallest task can become daunting. Track your progress, keeping a record helps.

Lastly, have you taken time to reflect at the end of the day? Moments of reflection are known to be therapeutic. It marks the end of a period, so you can embrace the next. Take some time to document what is working and what is not working.

_____

_____

_____

_____

If you need assistance on being consistent, resources are available in the back of this journal

Let's Go!

Let's continue to move forward and reflect on your progress. At this point you are gaining momentum that is undeniable. Time to amplify that and analyze it below:

What scripture did you connect with the most this week? Why?

_____

_____

What were your wins for the week? What were you able to complete?

_____

_____

What are you grateful for going into next week?

_____

_____

You have week two under your belt.

We are halfway through this experience

WEEK 2 COMPLETE

DAY 15

He gives strength to the weary,

And to him who has no might He increases power.

Even youths grow weary and tired,

And vigorous young men stumble badly,

[31]But those who wait for the LORD [who expect, look for, and hope in Him]

Will gain new strength and renew their power;

They will lift up their wings [and rise up close to God] like eagles [rising toward

the sun];

They will run and not become weary,

They will walk and not grow tired.

Isaiah 40:29-31 AMP

GOD doesn't come and go. God lasts. He's Creator of all you can see or imagine.

He doesn't get tired out, doesn't pause to catch his breath.

And he knows everything, inside and out. He energizes those who get tired,

gives fresh strength to dropouts.

For even young people tire and drop out,

young folk in their prime stumble and fall.

But those who wait upon GOD get fresh strength.

They spread their wings and soar like eagles,

They run and don't get tired,

they walk and don't lag behind.

Isaiah 40:29-31 MSG

DAY FIFTEEN: MEDITATION

DATE: _____.

Take a moment to journal what this scripture means to you. Meditate on the text. I encourage you to read the entire chapter. How can you apply this text to where you are today?

_____

_____

_____

_____

_____

_____

_____

_____

_____

_____

_____

DAY FIFTEEN: PRODUCTIVITY PAGE

Take a moment to write down every task that may be on your mind during this moment. This section will be called the "Brain Dump". We will prioritize on the next column. In order to execute at a high level, prioritization must always be key.

Now out of that list of items that have been written down and off your mind. Prioritize and narrow down at least 3 task you can complete today!

Allow each task to be SMART. Specific, Measurable, Attainable, Realistic, and Timely (Complete Today). Don't allow yourself to be too ambitious, we achieve major progress by completing small steps daily. Once the task has been completed, check the complete box.

_____

_____

☐ Completed

_____

_____

☐ Completed

_____

_____

☐ Completed

DAY FIFTEEN: REFLECTION   DATE: _____.

Take a moment to journal and reflect on your day. You are getting ready to spread your wings and fly. (Isaiah 40:29 AMP) Let's take a moment to consider the events of today and document what occurred.

_____

_____

_____

_____

_____

_____

_____

_____

_____

_____

_____

_____

_____

_____

_____

_____

_____

_____

_____

_____

_____

_____

_____

_____

DAY 16

"For I am convinced [and continue to be convinced—beyond any doubt] that neither death, nor life, nor angels, nor principalities, nor things present and threatening, nor things to come, nor powers, nor height, nor depth, nor any other created thing, will be able to separate us from the [unlimited] love of God, which is in Christ Jesus our Lord."
Romans 8:38-39 AMP

Coach Kellie's Corner:

The love of Christ is a beautiful concept. I love this text because it explains that no matter what we face or what we are up against, God is right there. God's love is not intimidated by threats and trials. His love is powerful, relentless, and similar to a force field.

I've learned that when I can't trace God or see a solution to a problem, to lean on the concept of God's love. The principle that Jesus Christ loves me so much that he won't let me fall. His love is unconditional, it has no boundaries and no separation. Trust and rely on this concept today, Jesus loves you and there is nothing you can do, or anyone else can do about it. God's love is concrete, it is permanent and a done deal.

DAY SIXTEEN: MEDITATION   DATE: _____.

Take a moment to journal what this scripture means to you. Meditate on the text. I encourage you to read the entire chapter. How can you apply this text to where you are today?

_____

_____

_____

_____

_____

_____

_____

_____

_____

_____

_____

DAY SIXTEEN: PRODUCTIVITY PAGE

Take a moment to write down every task that may be on your mind during this moment. This section will be called the "Brain Dump". We will prioritize on the next column. In order to execute at a high level, prioritization must always be key.

Now out of that list of items that have been written down and off your mind. Prioritize and narrow down at least 3 task you can complete today!

Allow each task to be SMART. Specific, Measurable, Attainable, Realistic, and Timely (Complete Today). Don't allow yourself to be too ambitious, we achieve major progress by completing small steps daily. Once the task has been completed, check the complete box.

_____

_____

_____

_____ ☐ Completed

_____

_____

_____ ☐ Completed

_____

_____ ☐ Completed

_____

DAY SIXTEEN: REFLECTION

DATE: _____.

Take a moment to journal and reflect on your day. Remember nothing can separate you from God's love. (Romans 8:38-39) Let's take a moment to consider the events of today and document what occurred.

_____

_____

_____

_____

_____

_____

_____

_____

_____

_____

DAY 17

"The Lord will give [unyielding and impenetrable] strength to His people;
The Lord will bless His people with peace."
Psalms 29:11 AMP

The Lord will give power to his people.
The Lord will bless his people with peace.
Psalms 29:11 GW

Coach Kellie's Corner:

Let the weak say I am strong in the strength of the Lord. We live in a world that can and will drain you of your energy if you allow it. We must be intentional to guard our time and take inventory of the focus we place on people and things. I have often fallen victim to overextending myself due to my inability to say no to people. However, just as it says in the text, Jesus will give you strength to say NO. I still haven't mastered it completely, but due to the grace of God I have been liberated to finally say no to situations and people that are draining. The result of this strength and courage has been an overwhelming amount of peace.

Peace can mean to have freedom from disturbance, tranquility:
If you have ever felt the same, ask the Lord for strength today to make those tough decisions. The Lord is here to help you and empower you. You deserve to live in peace and freedom.

DAY SEVENTEEN: MEDITATION   DATE: _____.

Take a moment to journal what this scripture means to you. Meditate on the text. I encourage you to read the entire chapter. How can you apply this text to where you are today?

_____

_____

_____

_____

_____

_____

_____

_____

_____

_____

_____

DAY SEVENTEEN:
PRODUCTIVITY PAGE

Take a moment to write down every task that may be on your mind during this moment. This section will be called the "Brain Dump". We will prioritize on the next column. In order to execute at a high level, prioritization must always be key.

Now out of that list of items that have been written down and off your mind. Prioritize and narrow down at least 3 task you can complete today!

Allow each task to be SMART. Specific, Measurable, Attainable, Realistic, and Timely (Complete Today). Don't allow yourself to be too ambitious, we achieve major progress by completing small steps daily. Once the task has been completed, check the complete box.

_____

_____

☐ Completed

_____

_____

☐ Completed

_____

_____

☐ Completed

DAY SEVENTEEN: REFLECTION   DATE: _____.

Take a moment to journal and reflect on your day. If you need strength and peace, it is available for you today. (Psalms 29:11) Let's take a moment to consider the events of today and document what occurred.

_____

_____

_____

_____

_____

_____

_____

_____

_____

_____

_____

_____

_____

_____

_____

_____

_____

_____

_____

_____

_____

_____

_____

_____

_____

DAY 18

"The name of the LORD is a strong tower;
The righteous runs to it and is safe and set on high [far above evil]."
Proverbs 18:10 AMP

"GOD's name is a place of protection—
good people can run there and be safe."
Proverbs 18:10 MSG

Coach Kellie's Corner:

Unfortunately, we live in a time that is so unpredictable and challenging that the name of Jesus is beyond a necessity. It doesn't matter what country or continent you live on, it seems like chaos is everywhere. Yet, I am relieved that we have a strong tower in Jesus. Did you know that God's name is a place? How powerful is that! I often remind myself that I belong to Him and that literally His name is on my forehead. We are branded and protected by the Most High God. It can be easy to slip into fear after experiencing hardship and watching others going through life. However, remember the tower that's available to you, run to Him in prayer and worship. Experience the Lord in a greater way today by acknowledging His protection.

DAY EIGHTEEN: MEDITATION   DATE: _____.

Take a moment to journal what this scripture means to you. Meditate on the text. I encourage you to read the entire chapter. How can you apply this text to where you are today?

_____

_____

_____

_____

_____

_____

_____

_____

_____

_____

DAY EIGHTEEN: PRODUCTIVITY PAGE

Take a moment to write down every task that may be on your mind during this moment. This section will be called the "Brain Dump". We will prioritize on the next column. In order to execute at a high level, prioritization must always be key.

Now out of that list of items have been written down and off your mind. Prioritize and narrow down at least 3 task you can complete today!

Allow each task to be SMART. Specific, Measurable, Attainable, Realistic, and Timely (Complete Today). Don't allow yourself to be too ambitious, we complete major progress by completely small steps daily. Once the task has been completed, check the complete box.

_____

_____

_____

_____

_____

_____

_____

_____

☐ Completed

_____

_____

☐ Completed

_____

_____

☐ Completed

DAY EIGHTEEN: REFLECTION   DATE: _____.

Take a moment to journal and reflect on your day. Remember the name of the Lord is a safe place. (Proverbs 18:10) Let's take a moment to consider the events of today and document what occurred.

_____

_____

_____

_____

_____

_____

_____

_____

_____

_____

DAY 19

Then Ezra said to them, "Go [your way], eat the rich festival food, drink the sweet drink, and send portions to him for whom nothing is prepared; for this day is holy to our Lord. And do not be worried, for the joy of the LORD is your strength and your stronghold." 11 So the Levites quieted all the people, saying, "Be still, for the day is holy; do not be worried."
Nehemiah 8:10-11 AMP

Then he told them, "Go, eat rich foods, drink sweet drinks, and send portions to those who cannot provide for themselves. Today is a holy day for the Lord. Don't be sad because the joy you have in the LORD is your strength." So the Levites calmed all the people by saying, "Listen. Today is a holy day. Don't be sad."
Nehemiah 8:10-11 GW

Coach Kellie's Corner:

Did you know that God wants you to be happy? Yes! Contrary to what people may believe, the Lord wants us to live a life of joy and delight. The kingdom of heaven gets no pleasure from us being sad and defeated. It is the enemy's job to keep us in a place of misery and depression. Ezra reminds the people here in the scripture the joy of the Lord will always be your strength. Make the decision to be happy and content today.

Joy is a feeling of great pleasure and happiness:

Happy is a feeling or showing pleasure or contentment:

DAY NINETEEN: MEDITATION   DATE: _____.

Take a moment to journal what this scripture means to you. Meditate on the text. I encourage you to read the entire chapter. How can you apply this text to where you are today?

_____

_____

_____

_____

_____

_____

_____

_____

_____

_____

_____

_____

_____

DAY NINETEEN: PRODUCTIVITY PAGE

Take a moment to write down every task that may be on your mind during this moment. This section will be called the "Brain Dump". We will prioritize on the next column. In order to execute at a high level, prioritization must always be key.

Now out of that list of items that have been written down and off your mind. Prioritize and narrow down at least 3 task you can complete today!

Allow each task to be SMART. Specific, Measurable, Attainable, Realistic, and Timely (Complete Today). Don't allow yourself to be too ambitious, we achieve major progress by completing small steps daily. Once the task has been completed, check the complete box.

_____

_____

_____

_____

_____

_____

_____

_____

_____

_____

☐ Completed

_____

_____

☐ Completed

_____

_____

☐ Completed

DAY NINETEEN: REFLECTION   DATE: _____.

Take a moment to journal and reflect on your day. Remember the joy of the Lord will always be our strength. (Nehemiah 8:10) Let's take a moment to consider the events of today and document what occurred.

_____

_____

_____

_____

_____

_____

_____

_____

_____

_____

_____

_____

_____

_____

_____

_____

_____

_____

_____

_____

_____

_____

_____

_____

_____

DAY 20

Be strong and courageous, do not be afraid or tremble

in dread before them, for it is the LORD your God who goes with you.

He will not fail you or abandon you."

Deuteronomy 31:6 AMP

"Be strong. Take courage. Don't be intimidated.

Don't give them a second thought because GOD, your God,

is striding ahead of you. He's right there with you.

He won't let you down; he won't leave you."

Deuteronomy 31:6 MSG

<u>Coach Kellie's Corner:</u>

Believe it or not we all have an assignment and a purpose to fulfill within our lifetime. Every person on this planet has a divine reason to be here. Now whether we choose to accept the assignment or purpose, it is up to us. Intimidation can be a real factor many of us face. Yet, the bible encourages us to not be afraid of people or circumstances that oppose our destiny. God created you specifically for your assignment. He goes ahead of us and gives strategies to tackle any hardship that maybe pending in the future. He assures us he will never leave us nor forsake us. If you find that hard to believe listen, I understand. Often times it is hard to trust a new concept you have never experienced before. However, let's utilize our faith muscle and ask God for strength and courage to trust Him in a greater way. Be honest and sincere with him, he will help you.

DAY TWENTY: MEDITATION   DATE: _____.

Take a moment to journal what this scripture means to you. Meditate on the text. I encourage you to read the entire chapter. How can you apply this text to where you are today?

_____

_____

_____

_____

_____

_____

_____

_____

_____

_____

DAY TWENTY: PRODUCTIVITY PAGE

Take a moment to write down every task that may be on your mind during this moment. This section will be called the "Brain Dump". We will prioritize on the next column. In order to execute at a high level, prioritization must always be key.

Now out of that list of items that have been written down and off your mind. Prioritize and narrow down at least 3 task you can complete today!

Allow each task to be SMART. Specific, Measurable, Attainable, Realistic, and Timely (Complete Today). Don't allow yourself to be too ambitious, we achieve major progress by completing small steps daily. Once the task has been completed, check the complete box.

_____

_____

☐ Completed

_____

_____

☐ Completed

_____

_____

☐ Completed

_____

_____

_____

_____

_____

_____

_____

DAY TWENTY: REFLECTION   DATE: _____.

Take a moment to journal and reflect on your day. Be strong, He is with you.
(Deuteronomy 31:6 MSG) Take a moment to consider the events of today and
document what occurred.

_____

_____

_____

_____

_____

_____

_____

_____

_____

_____

_____

DAY 21

The LORD is my light and my salvation; whom shall I fear?

The LORD is the strength of my life; of whom shall I be afraid?

When the wicked, even mine enemies and my foes,

came upon me to eat up my flesh, They stumbled and fell.

Though an host should encamp against me, my heart shall not fear:

Though war should rise against me, in this will I be confident.

One thing have I desired of the LORD, that will I seek after;

That I may dwell in the house of the LORD all the days of my life,

To behold the beauty of the LORD, and to enquire in his temple.

Psalms 27: 1-4 KJV

The LORD is my light and my salvation. Who is there to fear?

The LORD is my life's fortress. Who is there to be afraid of?

Evildoers closed in on me to tear me to pieces.

My opponents and enemies stumbled and fell.

Even though an army sets up camp against me,

my heart will not be afraid.

Even though a war breaks out against me,

I will still have confidence [in the LORD]

I have asked one thing from the LORD. This I will seek:

to remain in the LORD's house all the days of my life

in order to gaze at the LORD's beauty and to search for an answer in his temple.

Psalms 27: 1-4 GW

DAY TWENTY ONE: MEDITATION   DATE: _____.

Take a moment to journal what this scripture means to you. Meditate on the text. I
encourage you to read the entire chapter. How can you apply this text to where you
are today?

_____

_____

_____

_____

_____

_____

_____

_____

_____

_____

_____

_____

DAY TWENTY-ONE: PRODUCTIVITY PAGE

Take a moment to write down every task that may be on your mind during this moment. This section will be called the "Brain Dump". We will prioritize on the next column. In order to execute at a high level, prioritization must always be key.

_____

_____

_____

_____

_____

_____

_____

_____

Now out of that list of items have been written down and off your mind. Prioritize and narrow down at least 3 task you can complete today!

Allow each task to be SMART. Specific, Measurable, Attainable, Realistic, and Timely (Complete Today). Don't allow yourself to be too ambitious, we complete major progress by completely small steps daily. Once the task has been completed, check the complete box.

_____

_____

☐ Completed

_____

_____

☐ Completed

_____

_____

☐ Completed

DAY TWENTY ONE: REFLECTION   DATE: _____.

Take a moment to journal and reflect on your day. The Lord is your light and salvation. (Psalms 27:1-4) Let's take a moment to consider the events of today and document what occurred.

_____

_____

_____

_____

_____

_____

_____

_____

_____

_____

_____

_____

_____

_____

_____

_____

_____

_____

_____

_____

_____

_____

_____

_____

_____

_____

Excellent Progress!

Some studies show it only takes 21 days to develop a new habit. Let's keep gaining momentum and maximize the results below:

What scripture did you connect with the most this week? Why?

_____

_____

What were your wins for the week? What were you able to complete?

_____

_____

What are you grateful for going into next week?

_____

_____

Welcome to the home stretch, push yourself next week

WEEK 3 COMPLETE

DAY 22

But the fruit of the Spirit [the result of His presence within us]
is love [unselfish concern for others], joy, [inner] peace,
patience [not the ability to wait, but how we act while waiting], kindness,
goodness, faithfulness, gentleness, self-control.
Against such things there is no law. If we [claim to] live by the [Holy] Spirit,
we must also walk by the Spirit [with personal integrity,
godly character, and moral courage our conduct empowered by the Holy Spirit].
We must not become conceited, challenging or
provoking one another, envying one another.
Galatians 5: 22-23, 25 AMP

Coach Kellie's Corner:

The result of spending true quality time with God should always be fruit. The power to demonstrate love and kindness should be a goal for every believer. I will never forget the strategy the Holy Spirit revealed to me to identify a counterfeit. There are always two factors that can help you identify an authentic person from a counterfeit. The indicators are time and fruit. Time will always tell the story as it does with jewelry, if it is fake, it will eventually turn green, or a different color. Also, fruit will always be the proof of a person's character and result of living everyday life. Is this person patient? Are they faithful to a person or task? We must observe this with others and within ourselves.

DAY TWENTY TWO: MEDITATION

DATE: _____.

Take a moment to journal what this scripture means to you. Meditate on the text. I encourage you to read the entire chapter. How can you apply this text to where you are today?

_____

_____

_____

_____

_____

_____

_____

_____

_____

_____

_____

_____

DAY TWENTY-TWO:
PRODUCTIVITY PAGE

Take a moment to write down every task that may be on your mind during this moment. This section will be called the "Brain Dump". We will prioritize on the next column. In order to execute at a high level, prioritization must always be key.

Now out of that list of items that have been written down and off your mind. Prioritize and narrow down at least 3 task you can complete today!

Allow each task to be SMART. Specific, Measurable, Attainable, Realistic, and Timely (Complete Today). Don't allow yourself to be too ambitious, we achieve major progress by completing small steps daily. Once the task has been completed, check the complete box.

_____

_____

_____

_____

_____

☐ Completed

_____

_____

☐ Completed

_____

_____

☐ Completed

DAY TWENTY-TWO: REFLECTION   DATE: _____.

Take a moment to journal and reflect on your day. Did you show your fruit today? (Galatians 5: 22-25 AMP) Let's take a moment to consider the events of today and document what occurred.

_____

_____

_____

_____

_____

_____

_____

_____

_____

_____

_____

_____

_____

_____

_____

_____

_____

_____

_____

_____

_____

_____

_____

DAY 23

But He has said to me, "My grace is sufficient for you [My lovingkindness and My mercy are more than enough—always available—regardless of the situation]; for [My] power is being perfected [and is completed and shows itself most effectively] in [your] weakness." Therefore, I will all the more gladly boast in my weaknesses, so that the power of Christ [may completely enfold me and] may dwell in me. So I am well pleased with weaknesses, with insults, with distresses, with persecutions, and with difficulties, for the sake of Christ; for when I am weak [in human strength], then I am strong [truly able, truly powerful, truly drawing from God's strength].
2 Corinthians 12: 9-10 AMP

Coach Kellie's Corner:

Truth be told, it took me a long time to receive any revelation from this scripture. I didn't understand how being weak or enduring hard times was perfecting God's power within me. It didn't make sense, until I realized that dealing with unemployment, relationship loss, and financial issues drew me closer to Christ. Walking through those difficult moments humbled me, they assisted me in taking my prayer life to the next level. I had to completely depend on God and only draw strength from Him. This is why the writer says "when I am weak in human strength, then I am strong and powerful in God's strength." This statement is so powerful. We must learn to tap into that unlimited resource and consistently draw from Jesus, the well that never runs dry.

DAY TWENTY THREE: MEDITATION

DATE: _____.

Take a moment to journal what this scripture means to you. Meditate on the text. I encourage you to read the entire chapter. How can you apply this text to where you are today?

_____

_____

_____

_____

_____

_____

_____

_____

_____

_____

_____

DAY TWENTY-THREE: PRODUCTIVITY PAGE

Take a moment to write down every task that may be on your mind during this moment. This section will be called the "Brain Dump". We will prioritize on the next column. In order to execute at a high level, prioritization must always be key.

Now out of that list of items that have been written down and off your mind. Prioritize and narrow down at least 3 task you can complete today!

Allow each task to be SMART. Specific, Measurable, Attainable, Realistic, and Timely (Complete Today). Don't allow yourself to be too ambitious, we achieve major progress by completing small steps daily. Once the task has been completed, check the complete box.

_____

_____

_____

_____

☐ Completed

_____

_____

_____

_____

☐ Completed

_____

_____

_____

☐ Completed

DAY TWENTY THREE: REFLECTION   DATE: _____.

Take a moment to journal and reflect on your day. Remember God's grace is sufficient for you. (2 Corinthians 12:9-10) Let's take a moment to consider the events of today and document what occurred.

_____

_____

_____

_____

_____

_____

_____

_____

_____

_____

_____

DAY 24

God, you're such a safe and powerful place to find refuge!

You're a proven help in time of trouble—

more than enough and always available whenever I need you.

So we will never fear

even if every structure of support were to crumble away.

We will not fear even when the earthquakes and shakes,

moving mountains and casting them into the sea.

Psalms 46:1-2 TPT

God is our refuge and strength [mighty and impenetrable],

A very present and well-proved help in trouble.

Therefore we will not fear, though the earth should change

And though the mountains be shaken and slip into the heart of the seas,

Psalms 46: 1-2 AMP

Coach Kellie's Corner:

One of my favorite names for God is Jehovah Shammah, meaning the Lord is there. I love it because it reminds me that He is a very present help in times of trouble. It helps me to continue to move forward in my goals or whatever I am facing at the time. It is a beautiful feeling to know God has your back. Although, people and circumstances may change, the Lord is consistent and always right there for you. He is our refuge, strength, a safe and powerful place for us to rest.

DAY TWENTY FOUR: MEDITATION

DATE: _____.

Take a moment to journal what this scripture means to you. Meditate on the text. I encourage you to read the entire chapter. How can you apply this text to where you are today?

_____

_____

_____

_____

_____

_____

_____

_____

_____

_____

_____

DAY TWENTY-FOUR: PRODUCTIVITY PAGE

Take a moment to write down every task that may be on your mind during this moment. This section will be called the "Brain Dump". We will prioritize on the next column. In order to execute at a high level, prioritization must always be key.

Now out of that list of items that have been written down and off your mind. Prioritize and narrow down at least 3 task you can complete today!

Allow each task to be SMART. Specific, Measurable, Attainable, Realistic, and Timely (Complete Today). Don't allow yourself to be too ambitious, we achieve major progress by completing small steps daily. Once the task has been completed, check the complete box.

_____

_____

_____

_____

_____

_____

_____

_____

_____

_____

_____

☐ Completed

_____

_____

☐ Completed

_____

_____

☐ Completed

DAY TWENTY-FOUR: REFLECTION   DATE: _____.

Take a moment to journal and reflect on your day. Remember God is our refuge and strength. (Psalms 46:1) Let's take a moment to consider the events of today and document what occurred.

_____

_____

_____

_____

_____

_____

_____

_____

_____

_____

_____

DAY 25

"The Lord GOD is my strength [my source of courage,
my invincible army]; He has made my feet [steady and sure]
like hinds' feet. And makes me walk
[forward with spiritual confidence]
on my high places [of challenge and responsibility]."
Habakkuk 3:19 AMP

Coach Kellie's Corner:

There is nothing like walking in the confidence given from the Most High God. Your walk and stance is different. Your posture when seated is elevated and your conversation changes. I can recall when I really begin to embrace the Lord's strength and courage, my pace changed. I had a sense of urgency to not waste time or energy on insignificant things. People started treating me differently because of the undeniable confidence that was visible and on display. As a result, promotion came with more responsibility and God, being faithful, made my feet steady to handle and balance all that came with it. He gave me the ability to jump over every hurdle that presented itself along the way. Let's all embrace this confidence in Jesus and allow it to transform our entire demeanor to represent His kingdom in a brighter way.

DAY TWENTY FIVE: MEDITATION   DATE: _____.

Take a moment to journal what this scripture means to you. Meditate on the text. I encourage you to read the entire chapter. How can you apply this text to where you are today?

_____

_____

_____

_____

_____

_____

_____

_____

_____

_____

_____

DAY TWENTY-FIVE: PRODUCTIVITY PAGE

Take a moment to write down every task that may be on your mind during this moment. This section will be called the "Brain Dump". We will prioritize on the next column. In order to execute at a high level, prioritization must always be key.

Now out of that list of items that have been written down and off your mind. Prioritize and narrow down at least 3 task you can complete today!

Allow each task to be SMART. Specific, Measurable, Attainable, Realistic, and Timely (Complete Today). Don't allow yourself to be too ambitious, we achieve major progress by completing small steps daily. Once the task has been completed, check the complete box.

_____

_____

_____

☐ Completed

_____

_____

_____

_____

☐ Completed

_____

_____

_____

☐ Completed

DAY TWENTY FIVE: REFLECTION   DATE: _____.

Take a moment to journal and reflect on your day. Remember you have the ability to jump over every hurdle. (Habakkuk 3:19 AMP) Let's take a moment to consider the events of today and document what occurred.

_____

_____

_____

_____

_____

_____

_____

_____

_____

_____

_____

_____

_____

_____

_____

_____

_____

_____

_____

_____

_____

_____

_____

_____

_____

DAY 26

"I will lift up my eyes to the hills [of Jerusalem]—

From where shall my help come?

My help comes from the LORD,

Who made heaven and earth.

He will not allow your foot to slip;

He who keeps you will not slumber."

Psalms 121: 1-3 AMP

"I look up to the mountains and hills, longing for God's help.

But then I realize that our true help and protection

is only from the Lord,

our Creator who made the heavens and the earth.

He will guard and guide me, never letting me stumble or fall.

God is my keeper; he will never forget nor ignore me.

He will never slumber nor sleep;

he is the Guardian-God for his people, Israel.

Psalms 121: 1 – 4 TPT

DAY TWENTY SIX: MEDITATION   DATE: _____.

Take a moment to journal what this scripture means to you. Meditate on the text. I
encourage you to read the entire chapter. How can you apply this text to where you
are today?

_____

_____

_____

_____

_____

_____

_____

_____

_____

_____

_____

DAY TWENTY-SIX: PRODUCTIVITY PAGE

Take a moment to write down every task that may be on your mind during this moment. This section will be called the "Brain Dump". We will prioritize on the next column. In order to execute at a high level, prioritization must always be key.

Now out of that list of items that have been written down and off your mind. Prioritize and narrow down at least 3 task you can complete today!

Allow each task to be SMART. Specific, Measurable, Attainable, Realistic, and Timely (Complete Today). Don't allow yourself to be too ambitious, we achieve major progress by completing small steps daily. Once the task has been completed, check the complete box.

_____

_____

☐ Completed

_____

_____

_____

_____

☐ Completed

_____

_____

_____

☐ Completed

DAY TWENTY SIX: REFLECTION   DATE: _____.

Take a moment to journal and reflect on your day. God doesn't sleep on his children (Psalms 121: 1-3 AMP) Let's take a moment to consider the events of today and document what occurred.

_____

_____

_____

_____

_____

_____

_____

_____

_____

_____

_____

_____

_____

_____

_____

_____

_____

_____

_____

_____

_____

_____

_____

_____

_____

DAY 27

"Don't follow after the wicked ones or be jealous of their wealth.

Don't think for a moment they're better off than you.

They and their short-lived success

will soon shrivel up and quickly fade away,

like grass clippings in the hot sun.

Keep trusting in the Lord and do what is right in his eyes.

Fix your heart on the promises of God, and you will dwell in the land,

feasting on his faithfulness.

Find your delight and true pleasure in Yahweh,

he will give you what you desire most."

Psalms 37: 1-4 TPT

"Do not worry because of evildoers,

Nor be envious toward wrongdoers;

For they will wither quickly like the grass,

And fade like the green herb.

Trust [rely on and have confidence] in the LORD and do good;

Dwell in the land and feed [securely] on His faithfulness.

Delight yourself in the LORD,

And He will give you the desires and petitions of your heart.

Commit your way to the LORD;

Trust in Him also and He will do it."

Psalms 37: 1-5 AM

DAY TWENTY SEVEN: MEDITATION   DATE: _____.

Take a moment to journal what this scripture means to you. Meditate on the text. I encourage you to read the entire chapter. How can you apply this text to where you are today?

_____

_____

_____

_____

_____

_____

_____

_____

_____

_____

_____

DAY TWENTY-SEVEN: PRODUCTIVITY PAGE

Take a moment to write down every task that may be on your mind during this moment. This section will be called the "Brain Dump". We will prioritize on the next column. In order to execute at a high level, prioritization must always be key.

Now out of that list of items that have been written down and off your mind. Prioritize and narrow down at least 3 task you can complete today!

Allow each task to be SMART. Specific, Measurable, Attainable, Realistic, and Timely (Complete Today). Don't allow yourself to be too ambitious, we achieve major progress by completing small steps daily. Once the task has been completed, check the complete box.

_____

_____

_____   ☐ Completed

_____

_____

_____   ☐ Completed

_____

_____

_____   ☐ Completed

_____

DAY TWENTY SEVEN: REFLECTION   DATE: _____.

Take a moment to journal and reflect on your day. Let's stay focused on God's promises (Psalms 37: 1-5 AMP) Take a moment to consider the events of today and document what occurred.

_____

_____

_____

_____

_____

_____

_____

_____

_____

_____

_____

_____

DAY 28

"You did not choose me, but I chose you.
I appointed you to go and produce fruit and that your fruit should remain,
so that whatever you ask the Father in my name, he will give you."
John 15: 16 CSB

"You have not chosen Me, but I have chosen you and I have appointed and placed and purposefully planted you, so that you would go and bear fruit and keep on bearing, and that your fruit will remain and be lasting, so that whatever you ask of the Father in My name [as My representative] He may give to you."
John 15:16 AMP

Coach Kellie's Corner:

There are over 4,000 religions that have been established around the world. We live in a time where there are so many options. I remember pondering one day, asking God in my prayer time, "with so many options how in the world did I find Christ?" Yet, the truth is I didn't choose or select Christ, He chose me. I didn't have the mental compacity nor the time to search through 4,000 religions. It was the power of Jesus that selected me and revealed Himself to me in many tangible ways that shaped my life for the better. I realize many may think that they chose Christianity, but the bible tells us this is incorrect, no man can come without being drawn first. Today I am thankful for God's sovereignty and grace to save and rescue His people.

DAY TWENTY EIGHT: MEDITATION

DATE: _____.

Take a moment to journal what this scripture means to you. Meditate on the text. I encourage you to read the entire chapter. How can you apply this text to where you are today?

_____

_____

_____

_____

_____

_____

_____

_____

_____

_____

DAY TWENTY-EIGHT: PRODUCTIVITY PAGE

Take a moment to write down every task that may be on your mind during this moment. This section will be called the "Brain Dump". We will prioritize on the next column. In order to execute at a high level, prioritization must always be key.

Now out of that list of items that have been written down and off your mind. Prioritize and narrow down at least 3 task you can complete today!

Allow each task to be SMART. Specific, Measurable, Attainable, Realistic, and Timely (Complete Today). Don't allow yourself to be too ambitious, we achieve major progress by completing small steps daily. Once the task has been completed, check the complete box.

_____

_____

_____

_____ ☐ Completed

_____

_____

_____

_____ ☐ Completed

_____

_____ ☐ Completed

DAY TWENTY EIGHT: REFLECTION   DATE: _____.

Take a moment to journal and reflect on your day. Remember God chose you. (John 15:16 AMP) Let's take a moment to consider the events of today and document what occurred.

_____

_____

_____

_____

_____

_____

_____

_____

_____

_____

_____

_____

_____

_____

_____

_____

_____

_____

_____

_____

_____

_____

_____

_____

DAY 29

"Have I not commanded you?
Be strong and courageous! Do not be terrified or
*dismayed (intimidated), for the L*ORD *your God*
is with you wherever you go."
Joshua 1:9 AMP

"I have commanded you, 'Be strong and courageous!
Don't tremble or be terrified,
*because the L*ORD *your God*
is with you wherever you go.' "
Joshua 1:9 GW

Coach Kellie's Corner:

One of my favorite servants in the bible is Joshua. In this scripture God is reminding him of his assignment and that it requires boldness and strength. Joshua had the task of leading the Israelites to the promised land of Canaan. This particular land was known to be inhabited by giants and heavy opposition. Yet, God gave Joshua a supernatural strength and strategy to push the people to the next level. I want you to think about what your giant or opposition may be today. Remember God has commanded us to be strong and very courageous. This is not a suggestion but a command. Be strong and meditate on His word every day to receive His heavenly strategy, He has given us all enough to make it to our promise land.

DAY TWENTY NINE: MEDITATION   DATE: _____.

Take a moment to journal what this scripture means to you. Meditate on the text. I encourage you to read the entire chapter. How can you apply this text to where you are today?

_____

_____

_____

_____

_____

_____

_____

_____

_____

_____

DAY TWENTY-NINE: PRODUCTIVITY PAGE

Take a moment to write down every task that may be on your mind during this moment. This section will be called the "Brain Dump". We will prioritize on the next column. To execute at a high level, prioritization is the key.

Now out of that list of items that have been written down and off your mind. Prioritize and narrow down at least 3 task you can complete today!

Allow each task to be SMART. Specific, Measurable, Attainable, Realistic, and Timely (Complete Today). Don't allow yourself to be too ambitious, we achieve major progress by completing small steps daily. Once the task has been completed, check the complete box.

_____

_____

_____

_____

_____

_____

_____

_____

_____

☐ Completed

_____

_____

☐ Completed

_____

_____

☐ Completed

DAY TWENTY NINE: REFLECTION   DATE: _____.

Take a moment to journal and reflect on your day. Be strong and courageous. (Joshua 1:9 AMP) Let's take a moment to consider the events of today and document what occurred.

_____

_____

_____

_____

_____

_____

_____

_____

_____

_____

DAY 30

"Endings are better than beginnings.
Sticking to it is better than standing out."
Ecclesiastes 7:8 MSG

The end of a matter is better than its beginning;
Patience of spirit is better than haughtiness of spirit (pride).
Ecclesiastes 7:8 AMP

Coach Kellie's Corner:

The older I get I realize the ending of a matter is not really the finale; that the ending of the old is the beginning of a new. I used to be naive about new opportunities and environments. However, I now understand you can't bring old behavior and old thinking into new opportunities. That old behavior can contaminate and ruin a fresh environment.

Better is the end of a matter because as a result we gain more knowledge, and a clearer perspective on life. The experience alone helps us to endure and persevere through life and it cultivates strength. It pushes us toward maturity and wisdom to continue to grow into our walk with Christ.

DAY THIRTY: MEDITATION   DATE: _____.

Take a moment to journal what this scripture means to you. Meditate on the text. I encourage you to read the entire chapter. How can you apply this text to where you are today?

_____

_____

_____

_____

_____

_____

_____

_____

_____

_____

DAY THIRTY: PRODUCTIVITY PAGE

Take a moment to write down every task that may be on your mind during this moment. This section will be called the "Brain Dump". We will prioritize on the next column. In order to execute at a high level, prioritization must always be key.

Now out of that list of items that have been written down and off your mind. Prioritize and narrow down at least 3 task you can complete today!

Allow each task to be SMART. Specific, Measurable, Attainable, Realistic, and Timely (Complete Today). Don't allow yourself to be too ambitious, we achieve major progress by completing small steps daily. Once the task has been completed, check the complete box.

_____

_____

☐ Completed

_____

_____

☐ Completed

_____

_____

☐ Completed

DAY THIRTY: REFLECTION   DATE: _____.

Take moment to journal and reflect on your day. Remember better is the end of a thing than the beginning. (Ecclesiastes 7:8 AMP) Let's take a moment to consider the events of today and document what occurred.

_____

_____

_____

_____

_____

_____

_____

_____

_____

_____

_____

_____

_____

_____

_____

_____

_____

_____

_____

_____

_____

_____

_____

_____

Congratulations!

Congratulations on completing this 30-day transformational journal.

Amazing moments can happen when we keep our obligations and promises to

ourselves and each other. I pray this journal was a blessing and an example

that with God anything is impossible.

Additional Notes/Dream Pages: DATE: _____.

_____

_____

_____

_____

_____

_____

_____

_____

_____

_____

_____

_____

_____

References:

Business Review, H. (2018, December 11). *Working with people who aren't self-aware*. Harvard Business Review. Retrieved July 1, 2022, from https://hbr.org/2018/10/working-with-people-who-arent-self-aware

Read the Bible. A free bible on your phone, tablet, and computer. Read the Bible. A free Bible on your phone, tablet, and computer. | The Bible App | Bible.com. (n.d.). Retrieved July 4, 2022, from https://www.bible.com/

Resources:

Accountability Coaching Services: Ascension Life Coaching. First consultation is free, you can inquire by emailing kellieriley@itsbhfh.com or go to website www.itsbhfh.com/ascension

Other Books Written by the Author:

Be Fruitful: Time to Produce! *(Published 2020)*

Herman, the Lizard in my Mailbox *(Published 2021)*

ABOUT THE AUTHOR

Kellie is a speaker, author, certified mindset coach, and visionary who believes nothing is impossible with God. She graduated from the University of South Florida with a Bachelor of Science degree and considers herself a lifelong learner committed to learning something new each day. Her inspiration for writing this journal is rooted in her desire to see others win. Jesus is central to who she is and her mentality, and He is the reason she lives her life as a servant leader. Kellie is happiest when she is around her friends and family. In her free time, she loves to volunteer and serve her local community. She finds joy in being a voice of hope to everyone she meets and is a passionate intercessor (prayer warrior) at her church, spreading her enthusiasm for prayer deep into her community. Today, Kellie feels blessed to have the love of her amazing husband (Mario Riley) and son, who are among the most important people in her life. She is the co-founder of BHFH LLC (Because of Him, For Him) where she fuels her passion for spreading hope and encouragement around the world.

You can contact her at kellieriley@itsbhfh.com or find her on Facebook or Instagram @BHFHinc.

Made in the USA
Columbia, SC
30 August 2022